Away in a Manger	5
Andrew Mine, Jasper Mine	6
I Saw Three Ships	7
The First Nowell	8
Jingle Bells	9
Good King Wenceslas	10
Silent Night	11
While Shepherds Watched	12
We Three Kings	12
Once in Royal David's City	14
In the Bleak Mid-Winter	15
Jolly Old Saint Nicholas	16
See Amid the Winter's Snow	17
Ding Dong! Merrily on High	18
O Little Town of Bethlehem	19
O Come All Ye Faithful	20
The Holly and the Ivy	21
Sans Day Carol	22
Deck the Hall	23
Hark the Herald Angels King	24
We Wish You a Merry Christmas	25

Copyright © 2019 by Heather Milnes
First published in the U.K. in 2019 by
The Ashton Book Company
9 Dairy Farm, Ashton Keynes,
Swindon, Wiltshire SN6 6NZ
All rights reserved

ISBN: 9781694996947

Unauthorised reproduction of any part of this publication by any means, including photocopying, is an infringement of copyright.

ANDREW MINE, JASPER MINE

I SAW THREE SHIPS

Lively
English traditional carol

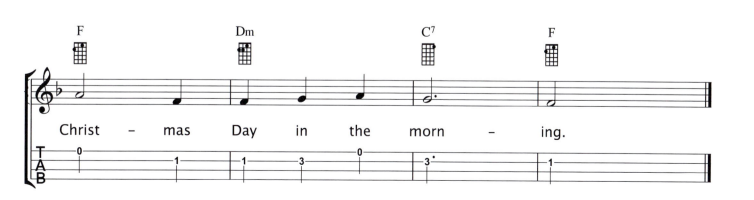

JINGLE BELLS

Quick and lively
James Pierpont

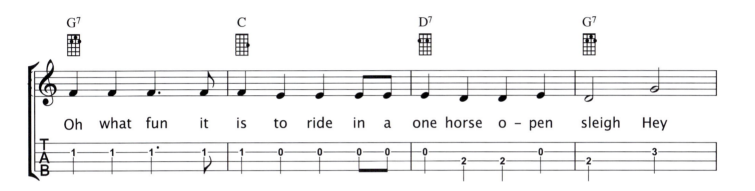

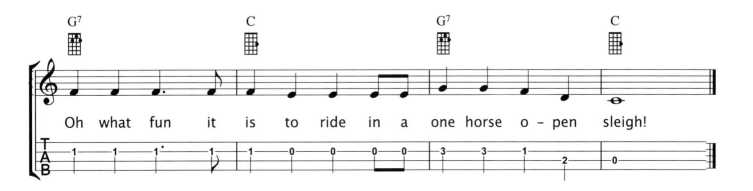

GOOD KING WENCESLAS

IN THE BLEAK MID-WINTER

JOLLY OLD SAINT NICHOLAS

American

DING DONG! MERRILY ON HIGH

Vivace　　　　　　　　　　　　　　　　　　　　　　　　　　French melody

THE HOLLY AND THE IVY

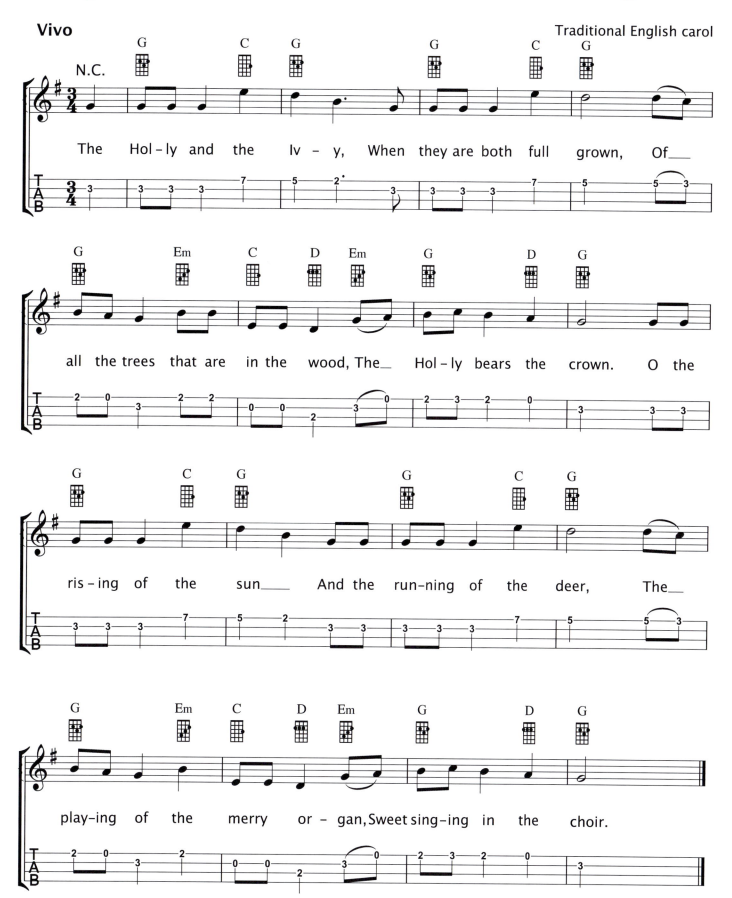

SANS DAY CAROL

Allegretto Traditional Cornish carol

DECK THE HALL

WE WISH YOU A MERRY CHRISTMAS

25

Allegro Traditional west country carol

Merry Christmas

CHORD CHART

MAJOR CHORDS

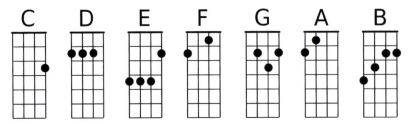

MINOR CHORDS

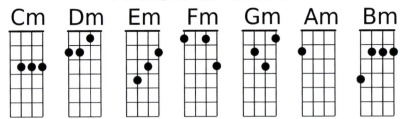

7TH CHORDS

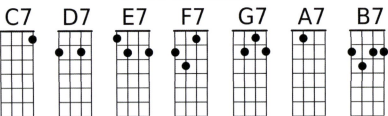

MINOR 7TH CHORDS

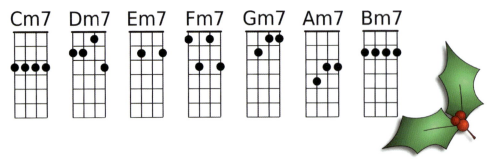

UKULELE NOTES ON THE STAFF AND FRETBOARD

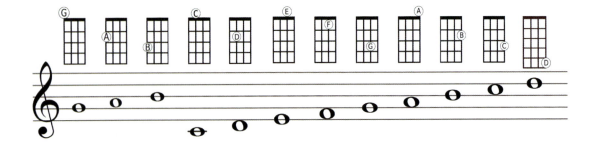

Backing tracks

Once you can play these Christmas carols you may like to try playing along to a backing track.

If so, you can listen and/or download backing tracks from
www.letsplaypiano.co.uk/christmas-carols-for-ukulele

Each of the tracks has a very short introduction so wait for a few seconds until that has finished and then start to play. You will soon get used to knowing when to start.

Printed in Great Britain
by Amazon